# Manga Drawing Books How to Draw Manga Characters Book 1

## Learn Japanese Manga Eyes and Pretty Manga Face

### By Gala Publication

Published by:

Gala Publication

ISBN-13: 978-1508598305
ISBN-10: 1508598304

By Gala Publication

# Table Of Content :

# How To Draw
# Manga Characters

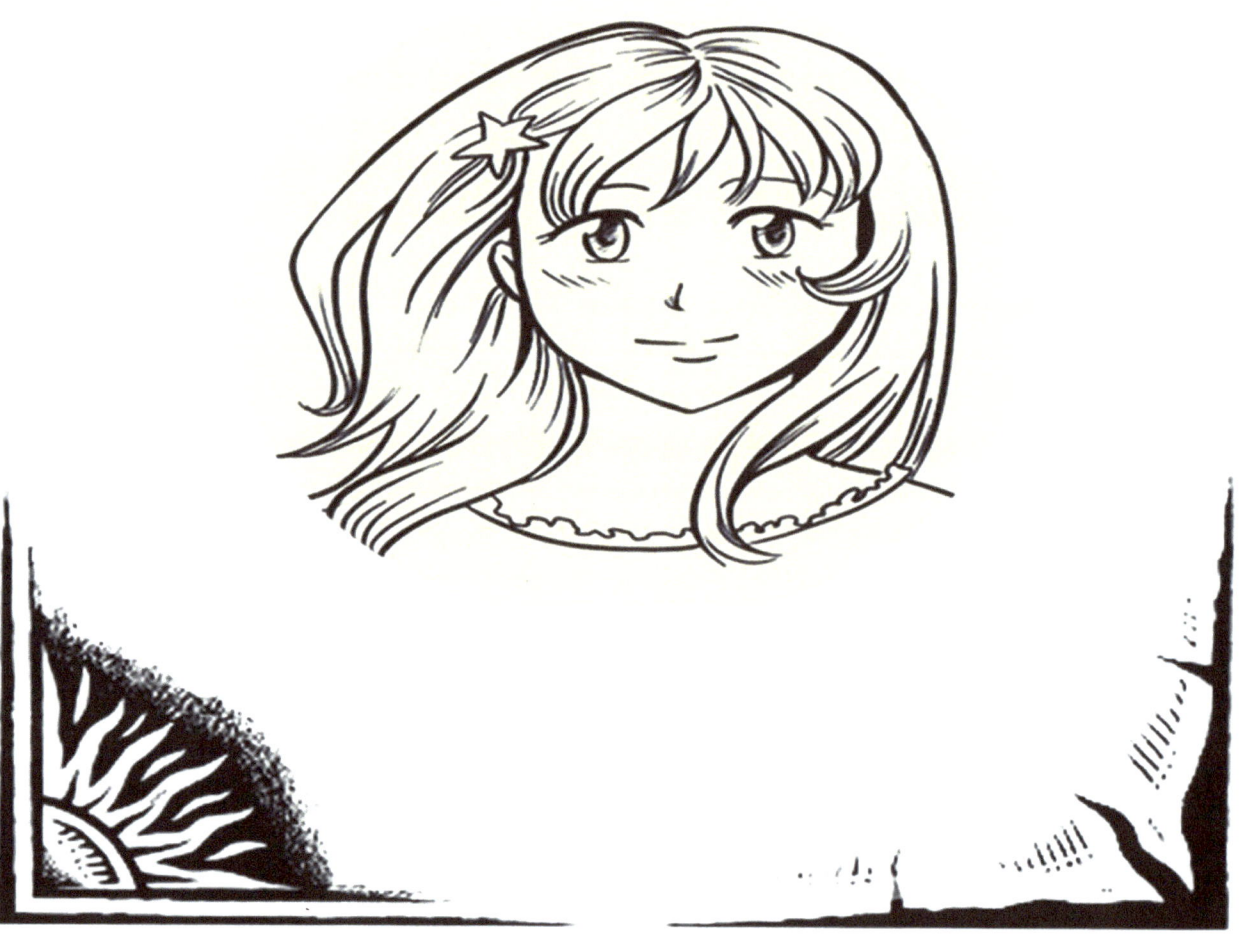

# Anime-Woman

STEP1

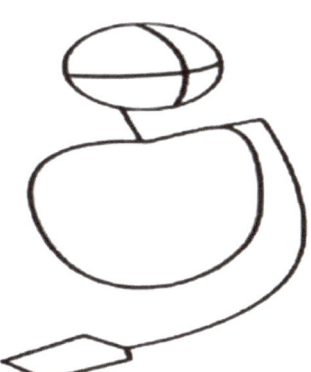

STEP2

STEP 3

STEP 4

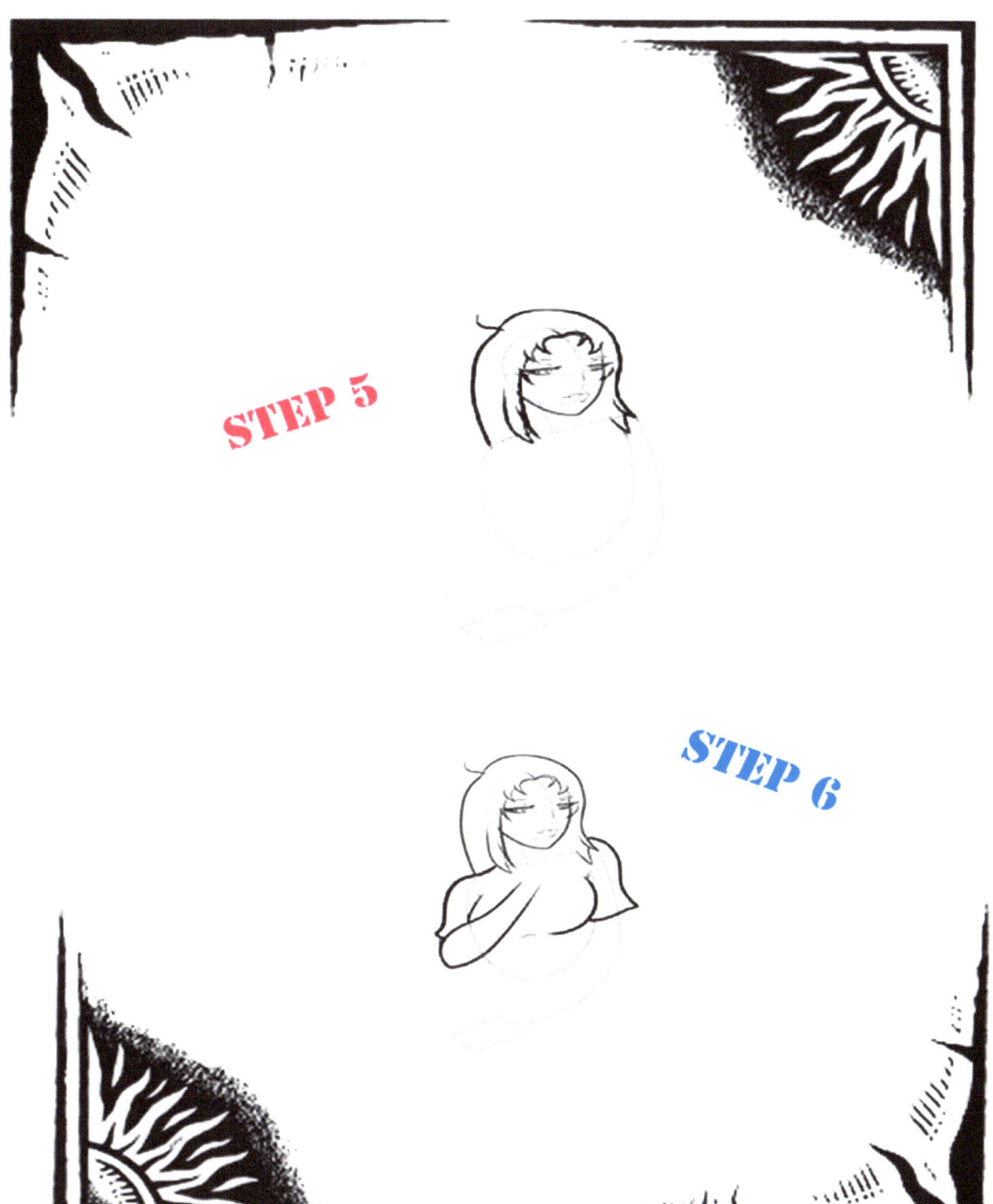

STEP 5

STEP 6

STEP 7

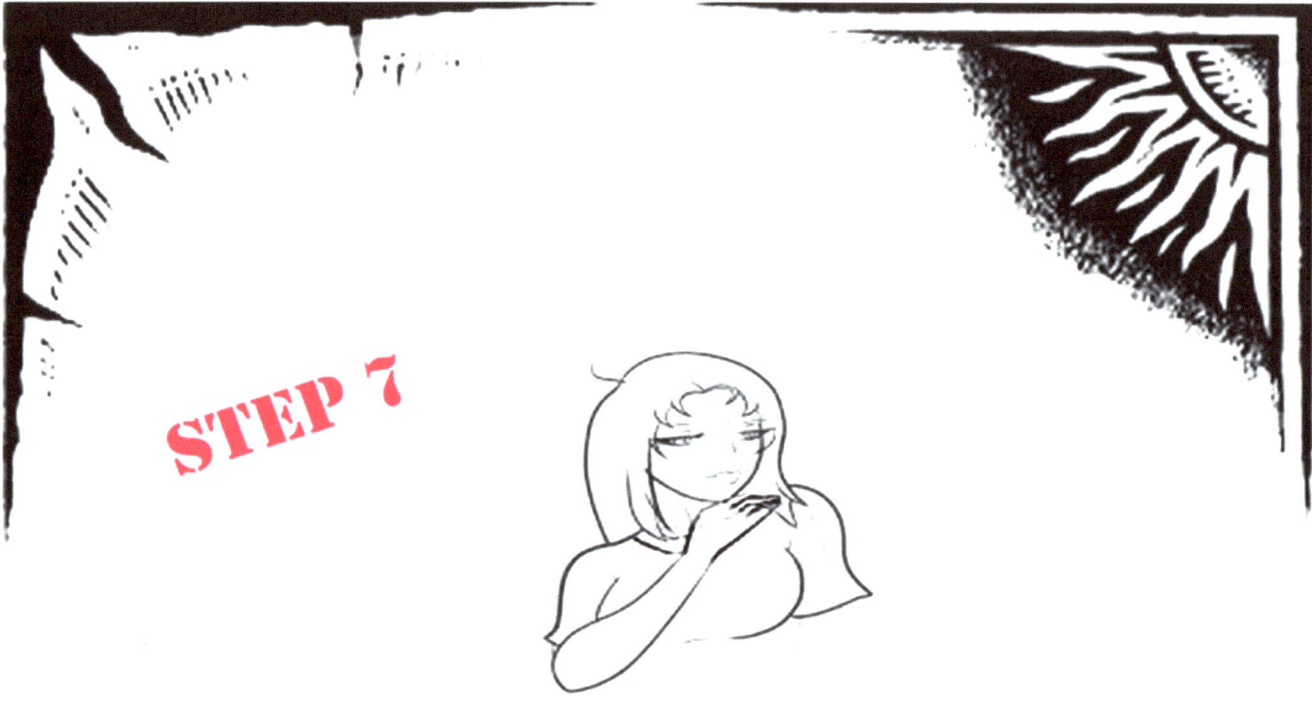

STEP 8

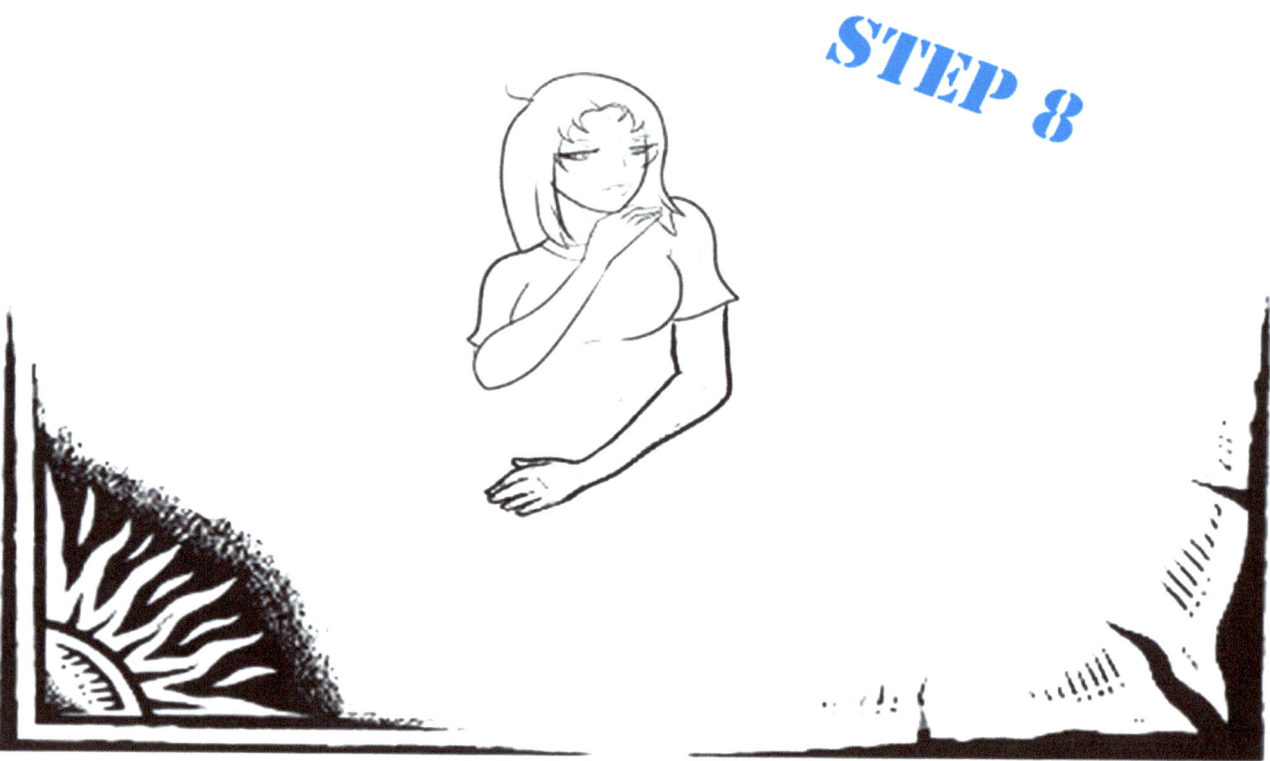

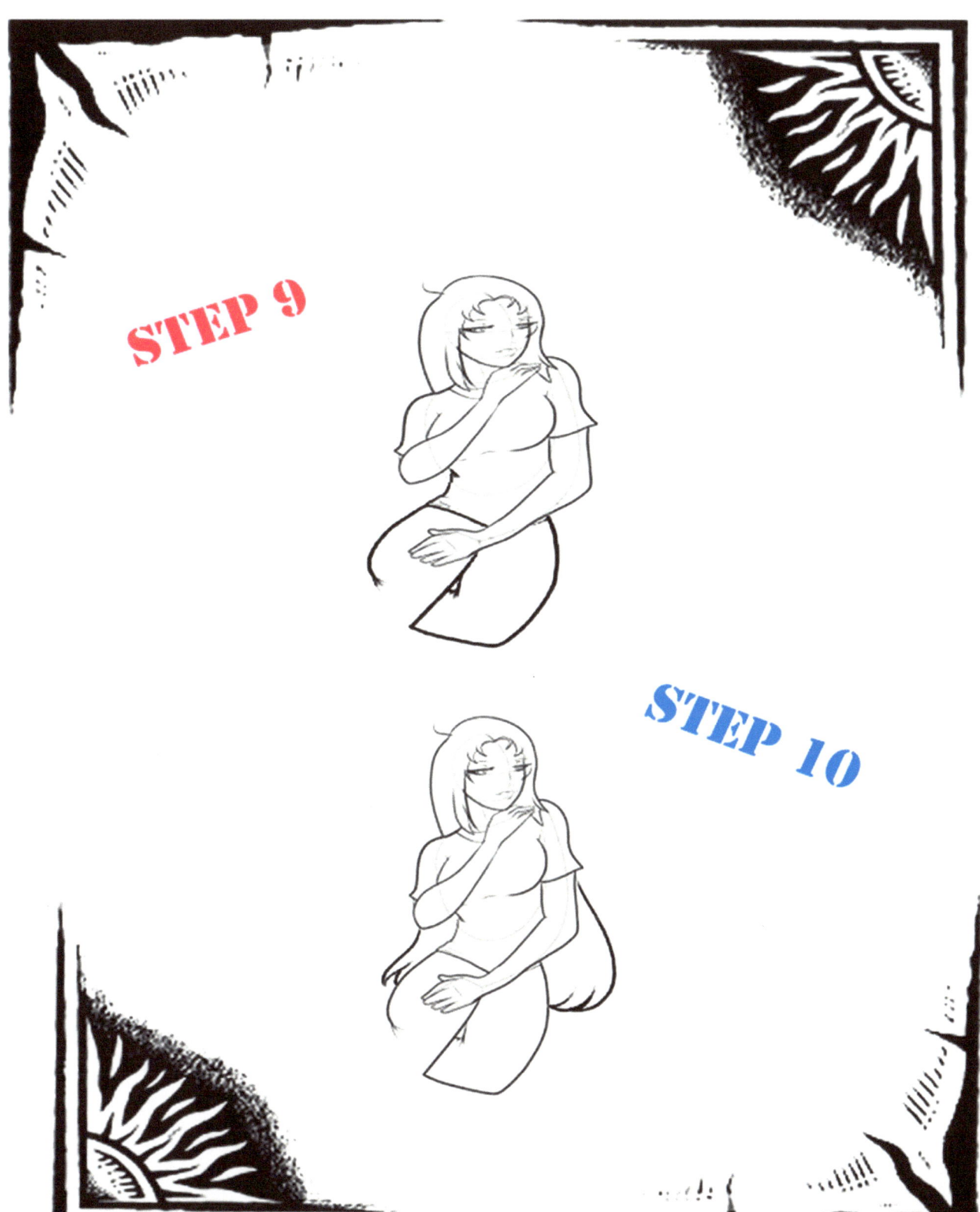

STEP 9

STEP 10

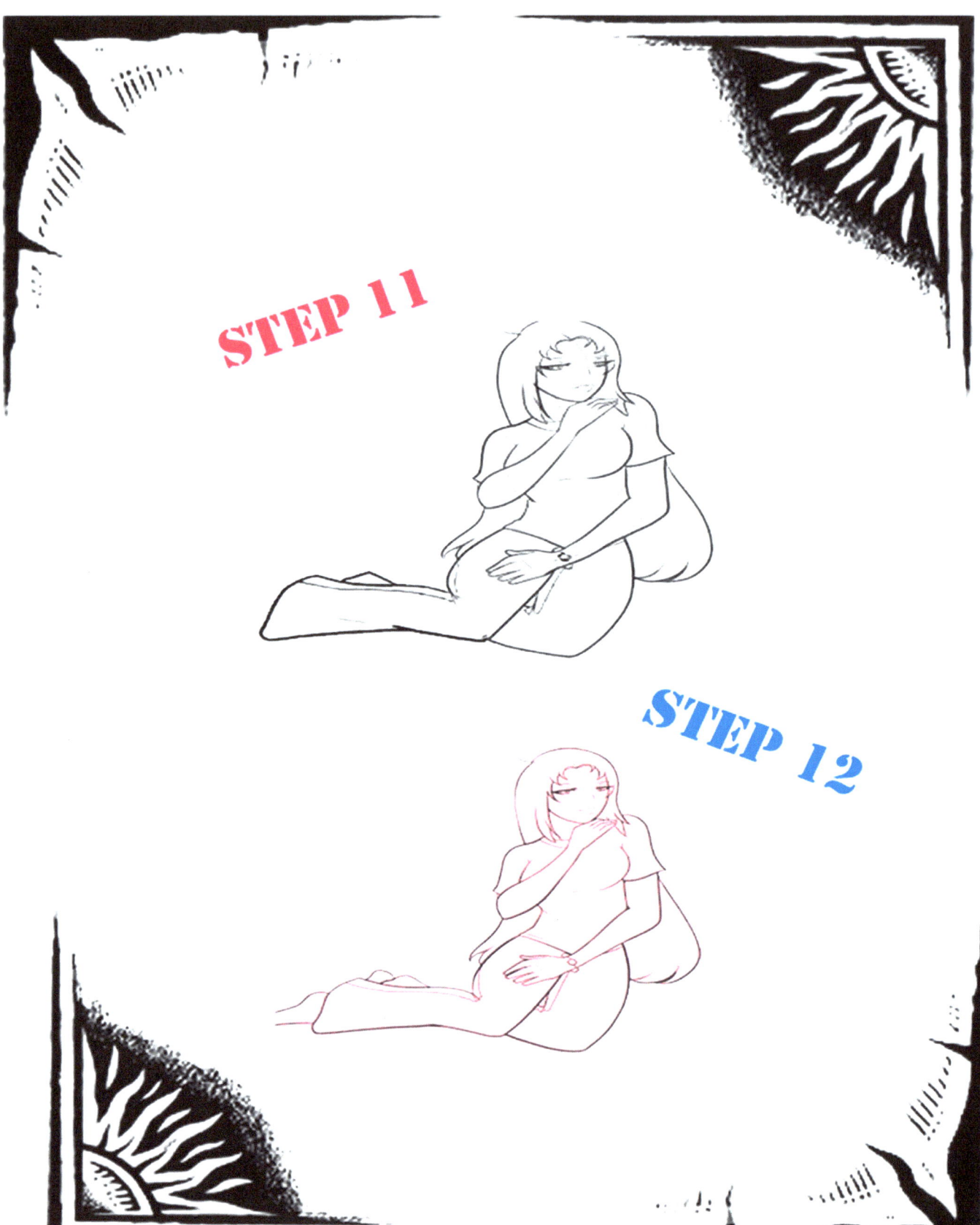

# Bishoujo

**STEP 1**

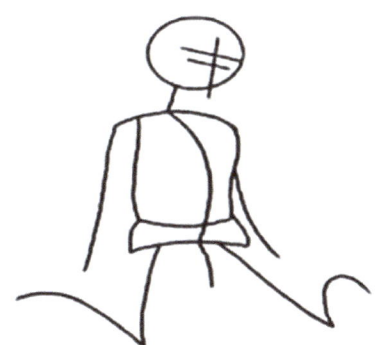

**STEP 2**

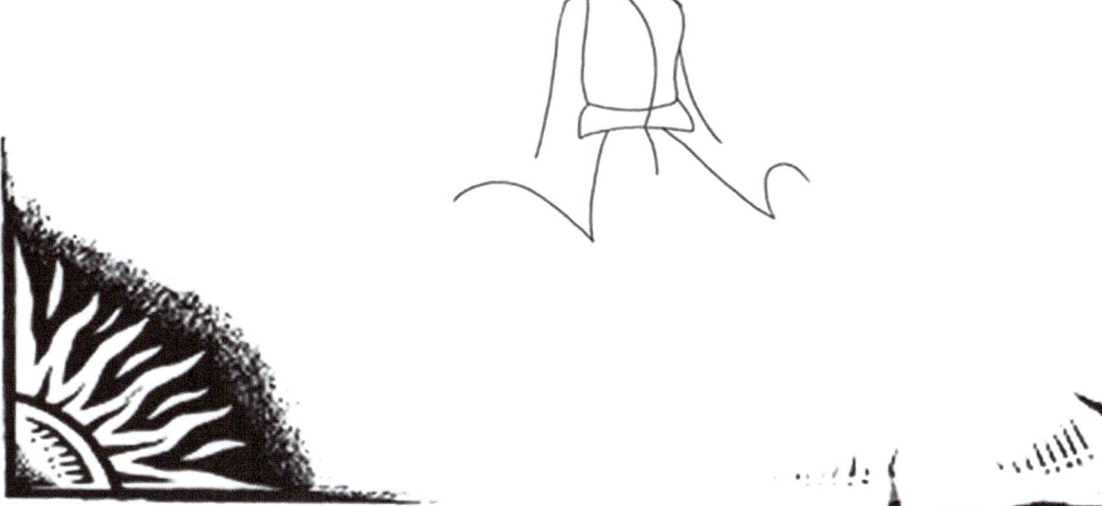

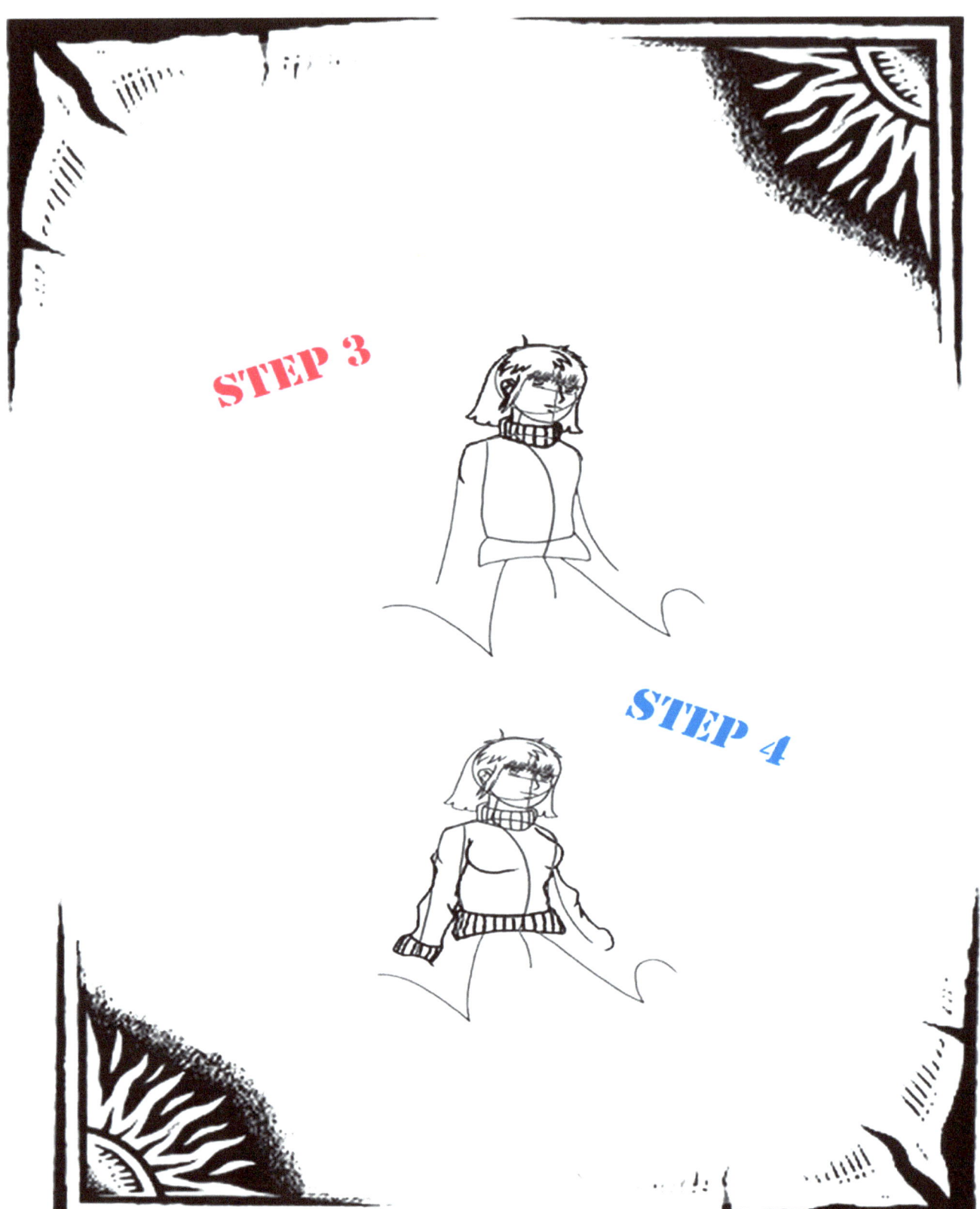

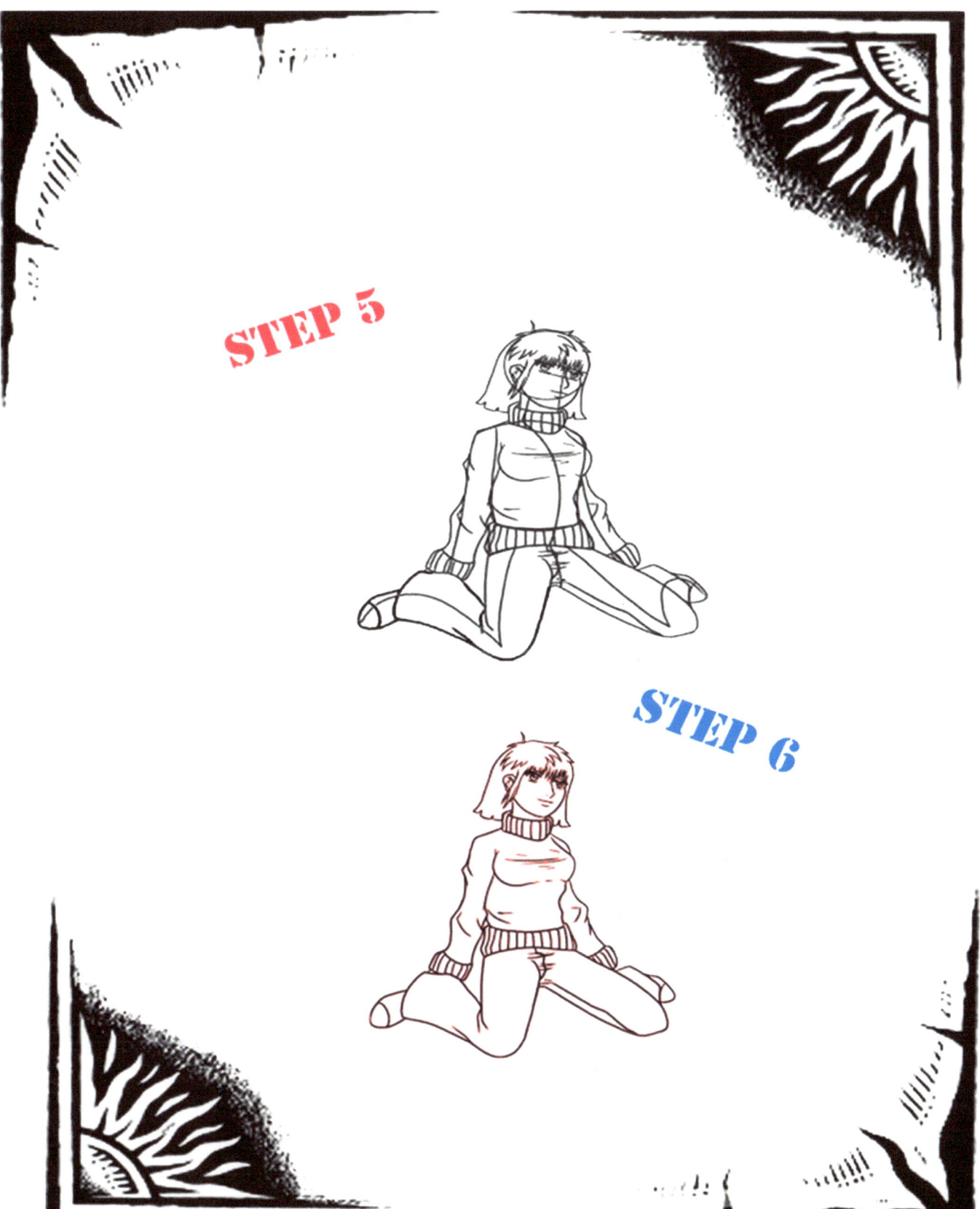

# Devil-Girl

STEP 1

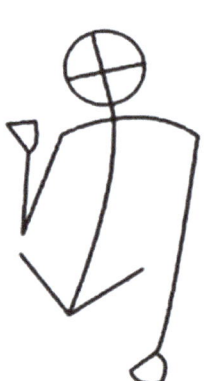

STEP 2

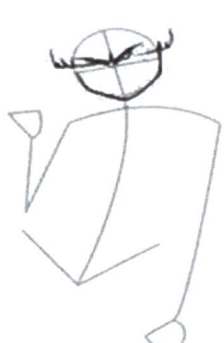

**STEP 3**

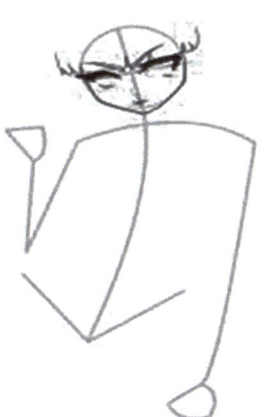

**STEP 4**

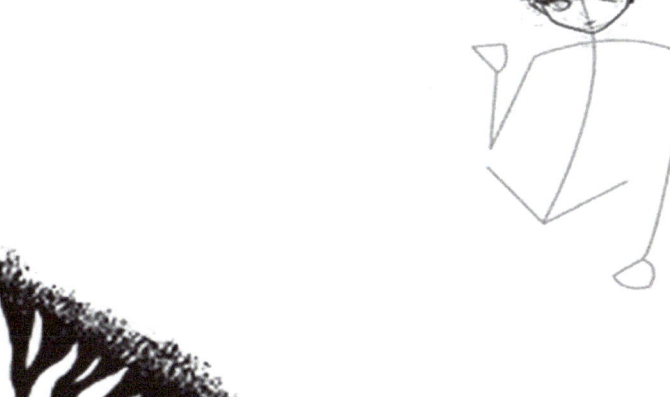

STEP 5

STEP 6

STEP 7

STEP 8

STEP 9

STEP 10

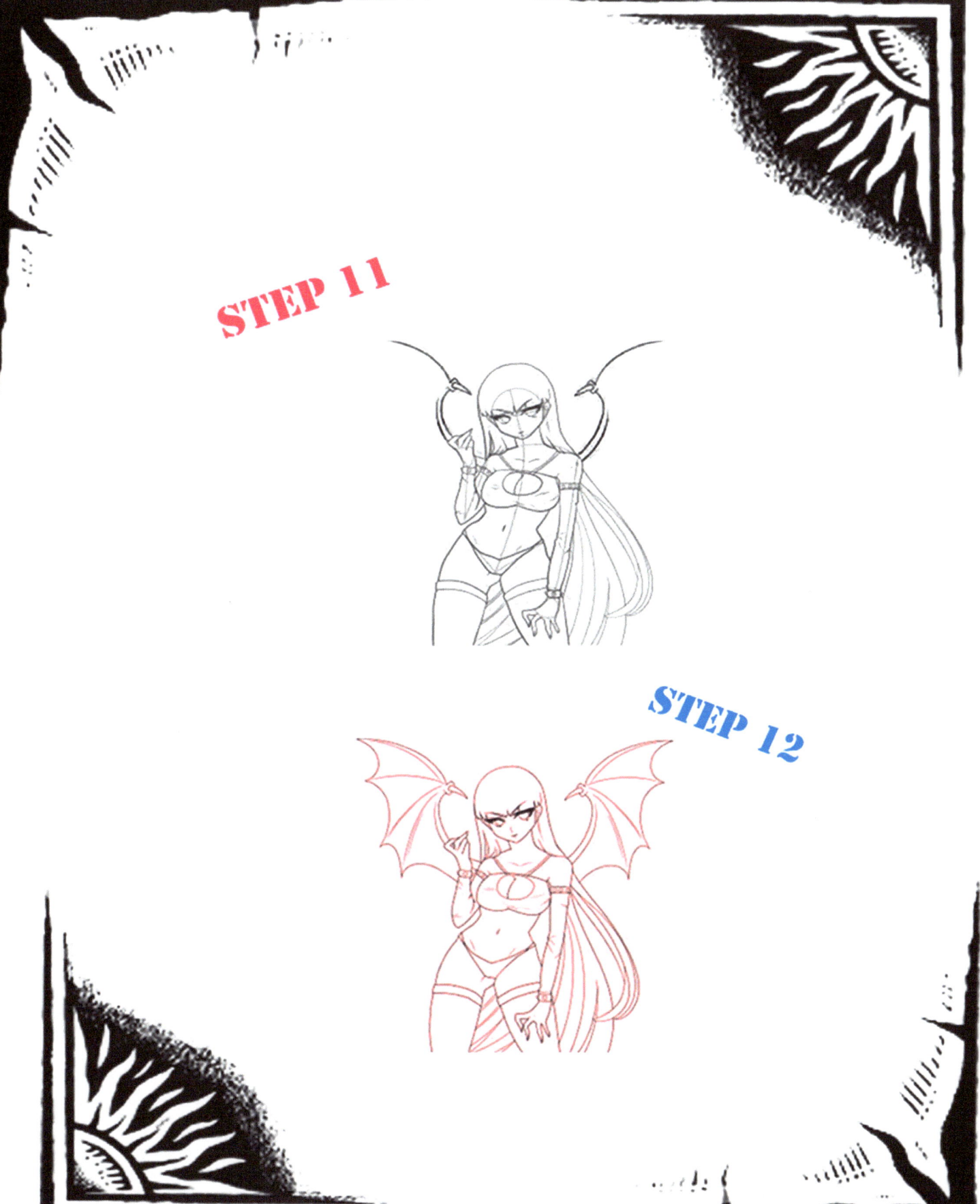

# Grape-girl

STEP 1

STEP 2

STEP 3

STEP 4

STEP 5

STEP 6

# ice-cream-girl

STEP 1

STEP 2

STEP 3

STEP 4

**STEP 5**

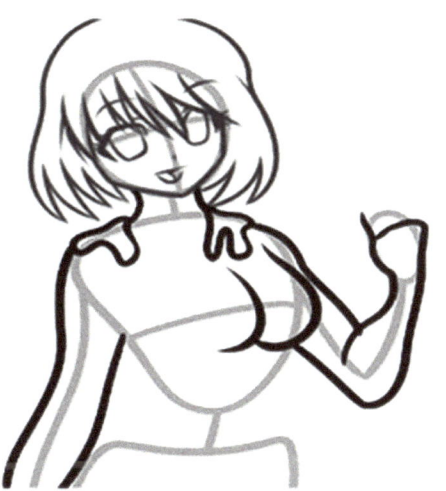

**STEP 6**

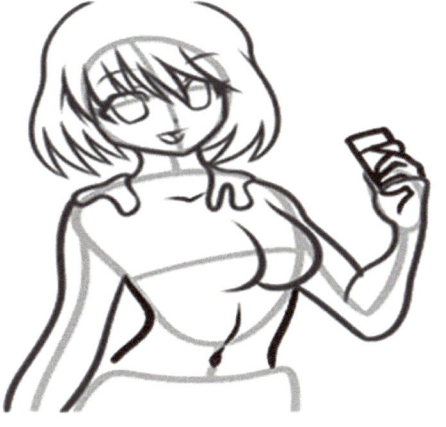

STEP 7

STEP 8

# kobato Girl

## STEP 1

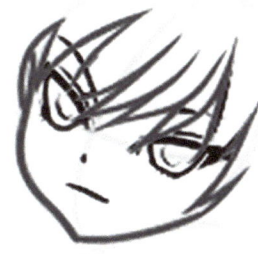

## STEP 2

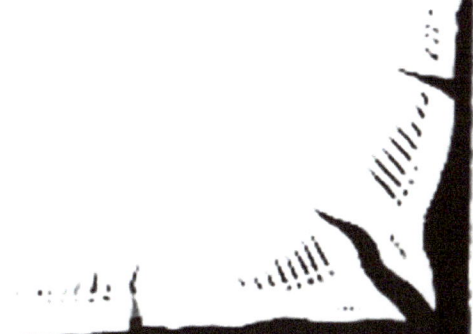

STEP 3

STEP 4

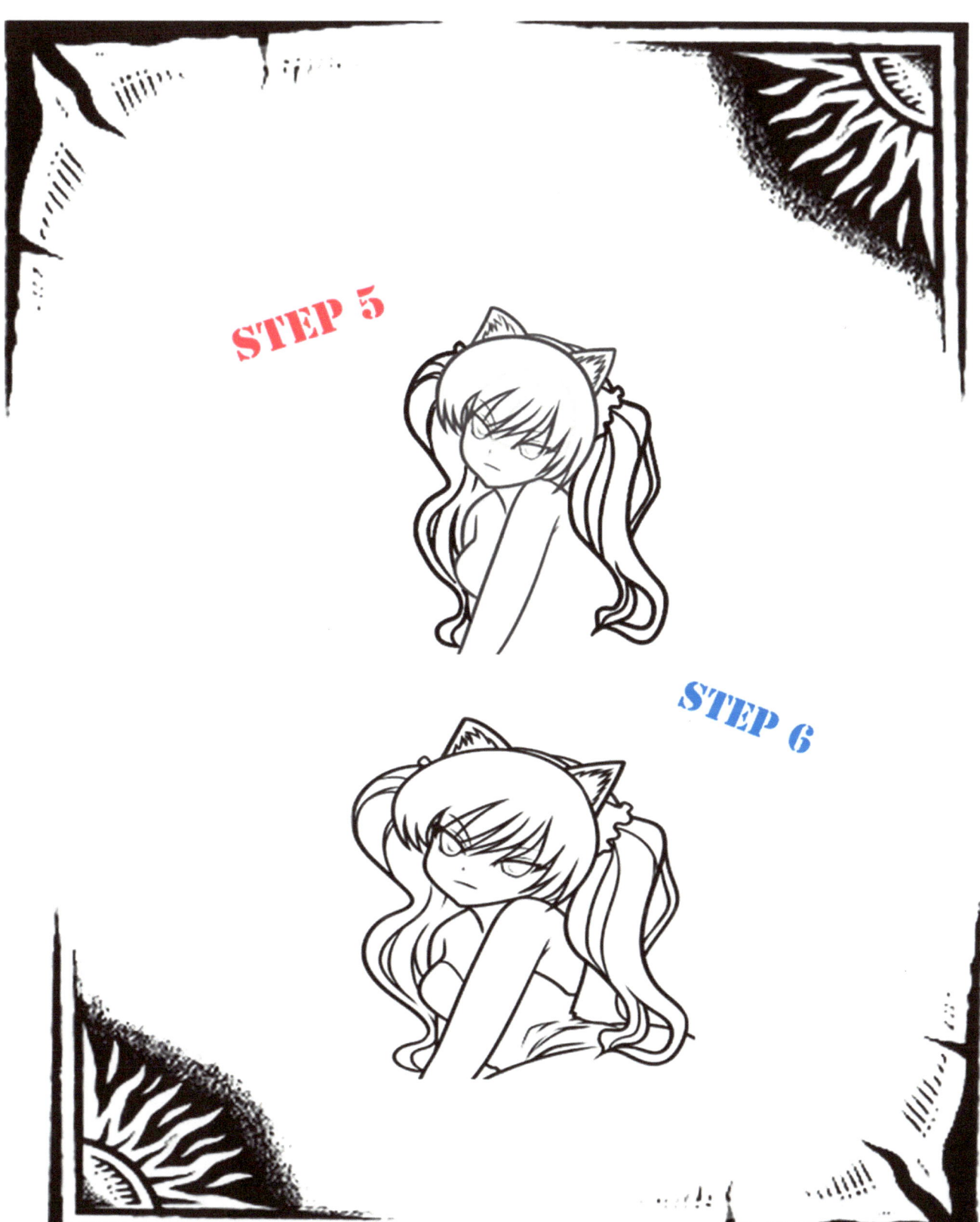

# THE END